A BRIEF BIOGRAPHY OF MY NAME

YALIE KAMARA

This is a work of fiction. All names, characters, places, and incidents are a product of the author's imagination. Any resemblance to real events or persons, living or dead, is entirely coincidental.

Published by Akashic Books
©2018 Yalie Kamara

ISBN: 978-1-61775-641-2

Akashic Books
Brooklyn, New York, USA
Ballydehob, Co. Cork, Ireland
Twitter: @AkashicBooks
Facebook: AkashicBooks
E-mail: info@akashicbooks.com
Website: www.akashicbooks.com

African Poetry Book Fund
Prairie Schooner
University of Nebraska
110 Andrews Hall
Lincoln, Nebraska 68588

TABLE OF CONTENTS

PREFACE
by Phillippa Yaa

There are moments in Yalie Kamara's *A Brief Biography of My Name* where the words disappear, leaving the reader with nothing but feeling, and the sound of their own breathing. Subjects of her poems grab the mike, speaking back to her. Her poems cross the distance between the poet's memory and the reader's mind, creating an intimacy that is not always pleasurable, even if always truthful.

A poet's creativity bends sounds and silences into meaning, always experimenting. A poem that is working captures in sensory detail the fabric of reality; suggests new interpretations and definitions of ordinary experience, responding to the abundance and the gaps in existing language. The poem embodies the shifting territory of self, the limits of the poet's sanity and comfort, marking transgression and *dis*-ease. The effect of this exploration is often beautiful.

Perhaps one's name is the first meaningful sound that we hear: folded into the shell of individuality, one's name is repeated countless times, flavored with intent and emotion, layered with various permutations of possession. Kamara examines this ordinary event in *A Brief Biography of My Name*, this pearl becomes a portal to memories of connection, of wrenching sorrow, of pride and delight, of terror and rage, a red thread through our unravelling historical moment.

As a first-generation Sierra Leonean-American, Kamara's investigation of her name resonates with cultures where the oral tradition embodies history, values, and everyday wisdom, connecting the past to the present, the individual to the collective. In parts of rural South Africa, children have to memorize the names of their forebears, their praises, or "mthakazele," and recite them at events where an individual's achievement is given back to the family, to the community, and kinship ties are affirmed and celebrated.

In a culturally diverse world, a meditation on something as personal as a name becomes a complex ritual of translation by a latter-day griot, for a community beyond language or race. In the title poem "A Brief Biography of My Name," Kamara narrates her discovery of the meaning of her names in notes and anecdotes, one from "a stranger who shares my mother's / maiden name, one that is not common / to where they are from." Although she relishes the link, she doesn't take the liberty of appropriating the man as family; while acknowledging the warmth of connection, Kamara resists a generalized, assimilated comfort zone in favor of the complexity of her unique life.

The violence done to "Me and my broken name" in "Space" is enumerated in elegant couplets that expose the threat of erasure that the immigrant has to bear, almost playful the final, uncoupled line: "the long-lost me, found the small, brown, I."

Immigration interrogates every aspect of the self and will always include loss: of home, relationships, and, perhaps most frighteningly, significance. As devastating as this may be, "A Brief Biography of My Name" challenges the poet, pushing a button as only a mother can: "As I write this, my mother asks why the village name matters if no one knows where Makorseh is. Maybe she is talking about me."

Unease creeps from the name into the body, to the feet nibbled by rats in "Pest Control" where "Not even the act of rest comes / without profound suffering." Kamara burns the effigy of asylum and reveals the moral fatigue of a society which offers paltry nourishment in "Repast in the Diversity Center."

Whatever ease she finds is hard-won. Although Yalie Kamara was born and raised in the USA, she grew up in a context that still uses the indigenous language of Krio, transposing an African sound and collective memory on an urban United States, gossiping about it, right there in its face as hinted in "Mother's Rules." In "New America," she is ironic, writing about the "Volvo / parked in an immigrant's daydream" and driving into the happy Hollywood sunset to joyfully accept "a Black that is steadfast and opulent," with all its complexity and pain, to arrive at the "careless twirl toward / where I think I may belong." In this map of displacement, the poet rewrites desperation and anxiety into their opposites with a rewarding and trenchant precision.

"Thurible" engages with religion and belief to meditate on the contradictory drives of nostalgia and claustrophobia that is family, that is belonging:

> I know that homesickness is born from distance
> and that distance cures home sickness.

Kamara's voice comes from a profound apprehension of the body in space, in time, constantly changing—changes wrought by nature, by danger. A black body in today's United States of America is vulnerable, yet Kamara is from elsewhere. Through the child's voice in "Sweet Baby Fabulist," she invites the reader to innocence, to stride across the world as god's creation, especially to admire and adore your black skin. The sense of wonder and inspiration is developed in "I Ask My Brother Jonathan to Write About Oakland, and He Describes His Room:" the threat is inscribed in the final line where "He finds himself too beautiful to not be in hiding."

Lush sensory detail materializes the everyday and stands as a protest against everything that seeks to erase it. The mundane bullet points itemize a magic realistic riff:

- Golden poppies sprouting between the novels on the bookshelf.
- Figs dropping from the tree attached to his door and rolling onto the cream-colored carpet.
- Wet fingertips caked with sugar for the hummingbirds flying out of his memory.
- A vine of thorns wrapping around the perimeter of the window frame so that they won't follow him home.
- The squad car driving past him, not using its siren to call his name.

Ultimately the poet's experience is that of a woman, the potential to nurture and bring forth life underscored with a clear and present awareness of mortality. Everywhere is the hint of endings, flickering vital life projected on the inevitable darkness. In "Soumission Chimique," she explores intimate violence in words and phrases that echo and amplify the silence that accompanies it:

> its hushed shrapnel exploded against

> every soft pink wall of me

The final poem, "Three Days Before My Baptism," demonstrates Kamara's economical, poetic genius, blurring the boundary between subject and author: ". . . It looks back at me, blinded // by the shower's steam."

Women are familiar with blood leaving the body in clumps, signaling endings. In a world where women are embattled victims, the poet is vital and alive with a childlike agency, able to engage with a present unbound by the past:

> I push it down with my toes through
> the drain. I step on the face of a nightmare that is smaller

> than my body, but bigger than time. Passed down from
> shadowed hand to shadowed hand, imperceptible in the

> charcoal bowels of my dreams, this is an ancient pain.

In a world where the village storyteller is a stranger to her context, to her origins, and in some ways, even to herself, the poems are a map showing the way home. Accepting the distinct social role of the poet-as-storyteller, as social critic, as word-collector, Kamara unpacks and measures experience and histories with a fearless vulnerability. She breaks down universal themes to everyday encounters that reconfigure the familiar and characterizes the streets of the US as her own—she affirms her kinship to her cultural identity and her political perspective.

Spare yet generous, the poems abruptly confirm a subtle, rigorous voice that responds to the benefits and anxieties of life in the USA as *other* with courage, compassion, irony, and faith. Kamara's voice emanates from the pages, recalling the oral origins of poetry; an affirmation of community; a sound that crumbles defenses and rationality; sure as a drum, as an instrument; from the opening poem until the last line dies into the silence that birthed it. This is life, given a proper and delicious weight.

A BRIEF BIOGRAPHY OF MY NAME

I. Djeli   Mende: blood.
                     Meaning, use the river in my vein
                     to paint a story that dries
                     the color of a bruise when meeting with air
                     and the passage of time.

Jelimuso   female griot, a story pulsing in every blood cell.

                     Francis Cole is a hotel porter who
                     is all obsidian and grin. On my last day in
                     Philadelphia, he tells me I am named after
                     a caste of West African storytellers.
                     He is a stranger who shares my mother's
                     maiden name, one that is not common
                     to where they are from.

Yalie,   I am made from the obsession of detail.

II. Sauda   Swahili: dark complexioned.

Fatat sawda   Arabic: black girl.

                                                            سوداء فتاة

                     When my father tells me that I am named after
                     my reflection, I think he's lying.

Saweda,   Who would wait so long to tell their teenaged
                     daughter a story that might save their life?
                     If I'd known at thirteen that they'd place a nocturne
                     between my names, I wouldn't have wished to skin the night sky.

I wouldn't have sought the sound of whiteness,
if I'd known that I was a song strained from indigo.
A note wrapped in lapis lazuli.

III. *Kamara*   Bantu: teacher; one who learns from experience.

~~Masuba~~   In 1945 (maybe), my grandaunt lops off my last name like a hand that has stolen. It is cut and left on the side of a red dirt road and disappears after sizzling under the tangerine heat of the Makorseh sun. As I write this, my mother asks why the village name matters if no one knows where Makorseh is. Maybe she is talking about me.

Nobody dignifies this loss with memory. I make myth for peace.

Masuba   I: one who gathers, in order to understand the weight of the hole.

SPACE

At the age of 7, a letter was plucked from my name
as a test to see who would catch the error. To see

who'd care enough to go search for the rest
of me.

For about 4 months, my name appeared as Yal e
on the page.

A part of me wonders why some names are sweeter than others
and become the nectar that pools at the base of our memory.

Would anyone let ssabelle, Rchard, Elzabeth,
or Snclar escape from the 9th letter of the alphabet?

Me and my broken name, less heavy than before,
began to float away to somewhere else.

No search party was sent to check between the
monkey bars, under the desks, my cubby,

or the palms of my hands. There was no red pen
to correct the flaw.

Nobody else played the game, so there's no
record of the joyful sound that was made when

the long-lost me, found the small, brown, I.

MOTHER'S RULES
For my mother

I. If you see me praying in the living room, never sit in front of me. You are not God.

II. When we go to a restaurant and I don't know any foods on the menu, never order me a meal that is spelled with silent letters. I came to eat, not to explore.

III. You didn't *make* food. No. God, did. You *cooked* food. Watch your English. Watch your faith.

IV. Your Krio is offensive. When you speak, you sound like Shabba Ranks. Your accent is funny, but keep practicing. It is the only way we will be able to gossip in peace while at the supermarket.

V. Try to learn the language of your lover and his family. They could be smiling to your face and getting ready to trade you for 6 goats and 3 mules during your first trip to their homeland.

VI. If anyone stares at you for too long (more than 5 seconds), start speaking an imaginary language while maintaining eye contact. They will be the first to look away.

VII. Consider the consequences of purchasing human hair wigs, second hand clothing, and used furniture. Maybe you will feel beautiful, and also save money, but you never know whose bad luck or misfortune will be sitting on your head, body, or in the home in which you sleep. Buy what you can truly afford.

VIII. Your father's Muslim, so you are too (1989–1993).
I am Christian, so you are too (1993–2012).
I am Catholic now, but you keep praying (2012–present).

IX. You laugh at me now. Like I laughed at my mother. Like she laughed at hers. Like your daughters will laugh at you. and I will live long enough to forgive your folly.

X. Just make sure to pray.

Amen.

PEST CONTROL

The *long mot arata* is a type of
Sierra Leonean rodent that strikes
its prey in sleep. It nibbles away

at its victims while they are nestled
in deep recline. Its teeth sand down
calluses until they reveal scarlet
and beige flesh.

Though its stomach collapses
under the anvil of hunger,
this mouse has principle.

It takes tiny breaks to purse its lips
and push a stream of cold wind onto
its target's feet, so as to offset any irritation
that may tussle the unsuspecting
out of slumber.

Though I don't know if anyone in my
family could positively identify the *long
mot arata* in a lineup of offenders,
their certitude of the mouse's
existence is irrefutable; it lies in the way

they express the betrayal they have often
felt at daybreak. They are disturbed by
the scene: short brown hairs flecked
on the bed and maroon paw prints inked
by their own blood.

Not even the simple act of rest comes
without profound suffering.

For most of my life, I have been haunted
by the tale of the *long mot arata*, and
taught to question my friends just like these
creatures, to doubt the admiration of anyone
who loves me without good enough reason,
to look for punctured heels following any
explosion of praise leaving a familiar mouth.

I had fallen many times from this spell:
the cool current passing over my toes
before seeing a bit of myself hanging
from your smiling lips. My wound, a
trace of your icy-breath desire to
take my feet and walk away from me.

I have gathered all of your forgotten
fur from my nightstand drawer and
plastered it to my body.

The moon makes an indigo silhouette
of your whiskers and snout.
Still and quiet, I wonder just when
you will notice how long you have been
eating yourself in the dark.

NEW AMERICA

Give me a kite that will twist its   leash in flight to   Oakland's sapphire expanse.
Give me   tradition   free from the thickness of horror: trick-or-treat
without my mother's fear of sewing   pins   and   sedatives nestled in the chocolate's
core. Give us some   good news: an edited issue   of the   *Oakland Tribune*
with every splayed corpse cut from its pages.   Nimble fingers to make   papel picado
from   newspapers.   Christmas or Ramadan.   Religion that will not leave me
questioned.   A dance and song that make   me   too lovable to hurt.   Shears to cut
the tightrope umbilical cord.   A flag whose fabric I can read.   Liberty or
its   synonym.   Give me   smelling salts to quell   this leg of the Atlantic
voyage.   Give me sunscreen   for my face and arms,   a sturdy cradle
rocking   me back and forth   at   the shore   of the Pacific.
A lullabye.   A hush. Whisper with ocean breath that this is   mine.   Give me a torch
to melt all   of the pennies   saved to buy this   Volvo
parked in an   immigrant's daydream.   Give me an   onyx   Cutlass Supreme
blaring Donny Hathaway from its cushioned innards.   Anthems   to sing
in a language   that I want as   my own. A Black that is steadfast and opulent.
Which is to say dangerous and infinite.   Give me a voice that will not remind my
parents of   their homesickness. Or maybe earplugs,   paper and a
pen. Give me a quiet home.   Give me a new America.   Give our family hands
that aren't scraped   raw   by passport page edges.   Give me a new America.
Or a new me. Give me a land mass   that reeks of   apple pie and bleach.
A silent pledge of allegiance.   Give me a license at sixteen.   Wheels and gas
and a hula girl rocking on my dashboard.   A hail Mary. With no map.
A minute to escape the sound of my misshapen name surfing off   the cliff of
every tongue.   A minute to drive towards the blue,   a careless twirl toward
where I think I may belong.

REPAST IN THE DIVERSITY CENTER

We line up with our paper plates in hand: two pieces of white bread, packs
of mayo, mustard and ketchup. There are tongs to grab the fixings: water runs

down the spine of the washed lettuce; it arches like a back snapping
out of a nightmare. Sliced tomatoes bleed into the foil pan holding them.

The Spicy Nacho Doritos rubs against the pink ripple of meat peeking
from between the bread slices. After every two or three deaths,

we are invited to grieve-eat ham sandwiches. I sit at a roundtable
and struggle to open my bag of chips between each microphoned voice

that laments another loss. How we've come together once more to eat
all that we cannot bury.

A man holds the mic like an ice cream cone:
"I mean, I guess I'd be willing to die if I had to."

He tugs at the bottom of his untucked purple polo shirt.
I thought the food would taste better.

When I am sad, the noises in my head are louder. In my mouth,
the chips sound like someone walking on loose gravel. My people

need to *crunch* up. It's *crunch* or never. I'd rather *crunch* on my feet
than live on my knees. It seems I might miss the revolution eating

state-sponsored food. A white woman from the campus mental health clinic
offers counseling services. She stutters, then fades into the wall as if to make

space for Marvin as he croons his famed question into the speakers.
I'll tell you what's going on: the lemonade is too sweet for such an occasion.

I'd rather drink water. Cheesy stardust bruises the tips of my fingers.
It smears onto any surface I touch. I am marked. Lord, people are dying

and the only evidence of my mourning are these party hands.
What a bright color against these deep black blues.

I have to be honest: I only came because I was hungry.

I ASK MY BROTHER JONATHAN TO WRITE ABOUT OAK-LAND, AND HE DESCRIBES HIS ROOM:

For D.R.

- *Night*, *The Wretched of the Earth* and *This Is How You Lose Her* on his desk.
- The yellow legal pad with the line drawn down the center. Pros and cons of attending either Stanford or Columbia.
- Pearlescent sunlight pushing through the blinds and slicing stripes on bed and body.
- How tiny tomato sauce splotches and the remaining angel hair noodles look like Pollock's *Number 17, 1949* against the white lunch plate.
- The arm that tick-ticks around the silhouette of the Jumpman clock.

I wait for fire to burst once again between the hands of this chocolate wunderkind. For electricity to dance through the fingers of a young poet. Instead, Jonathan offers me an inventory of his possessions. And I wonder why he's chosen the words that do not breathe a kaleidoscopic fury into the city scape's slate hue.

At the bottom of the message, he includes the parts of his body that he's most proud to own:

- Cinnamon hands. Straight teeth. An orange wedge smile. Peace between his left and right brain. A heart that isn't afraid of either side. A perfect canvas of skin.

Jonathan will not write about Mandana Boulevard and the six photos he took of the lady's garden before she called the police.

Jonathan imagines:

- Golden poppies sprouting between the novels on the bookshelf.
- Figs dropping from the tree attached to his door and rolling onto the cream-colored carpet.
- Wet fingertips caked with sugar for the hummingbirds flying out of his memory.
- A vine of thorns wrapping around the perimeter of the window frame so that they won't follow him home.
- The squad car driving past him, not using its siren to call his name.

He has no reason to leave his house if the most forgiving parts of the city are rendered in his dream.

Jonathan is creating a new town, where a young black man lives in a garden. Where his body is unfettered by the terror of others' imagination: when he hugs his own flesh, the X his arms make across his chest is not mistaken for a target.

He finds himself too beautiful to not be in hiding.

SWEET BABY FABULIST

For my nephew Elijah

In the third year of Elijah's life, black olives were black.
And green olives were black too. Even the bubbling pot

of sunset-colored palm oil and plasas was given the name black
soup. He so adored Tolee the koala, that he'd watch *Ni Hao Kai-Lan* every

noon. Tolee was no longer just a koala, but now a black
koala too. Black was the boy Elijah,

and his finger tugging at heaven for fire. Black
were his dimpled knuckles when he pressed his hands to pray. Black

was the hue of the world he desired, the color that would appear when he
rubbed his anointing oil on all that made him smile throughout the day. Black

is what he called the world, because he heard it from his black
mother. Black is what he called the universe,

to show us how much he loved her. Black
were the rainbows, the full moon, and the deep nightfall.

Black were the rivers and sky. God was as black
as the autumn breeze's call. Black

was as crisp as the crust of sweet potato pie. Black
was a brilliant, pulsing light—too bright to be ignored. Black

sings the joyful chest from which all fears have been unmoored.
Black is the sight of a little boy finding his reflection in all things. Black

is what a little boy called us, so what else could we sing? If black
is the chorus, an eternal echo of this one word song,

then what is the color in the hollow of the mouth that would tell
him that all he is living is wrong?

THURIBLE

"I'll be loving you until the day that you are me and I am you."
—Stevie Wonder

I know that homesickness is born from distance
and that distance cures home sickness.

And that rage is a big calcified hut of a heart
with one door, two rooms and a half-opened

window. And that you both sleep on
its floor when words are two mouths

full of broken teeth. And that this is a lineage thing.
From mother to daughter. I know that you will awaken

for two reasons: the whistle pitch of a ready kettle
on the stove or the fragrance of braided flowers swaying

at the lip of the open window. Today in Indiana,
I felt heat rising from my pulse points.

I spritzed both of your birthday present perfumes
onto my body as if they would never run out.

Lovely. I rubbed them into my wrists until my bracelets
clanged like laughter. *J'adore.*

Until I was joyful and almost bare boned. Until I saw
the human smoke of my good work.

Until my arms were incense. Until your gifts lifted
from my skin and glided on winter air, returning to you.

Until you dreamt, until you couldn't. And you both
arrive in the kitchen and drink hot water.

And talk about the familiar scent of kin set aflame.

SOUMISSION CHIMIQUE

I must have looked too pathetic to jack. Like the kind of woman that
even a thief has mercy for, simply because it appears that so much

has already been taken from her.

In the half of the metro ride that I remember, I see a sliver of
my brown body between the slow-motion flutter of heavy eyelids.

The train jerks back and forth until what used to
be beer in my stomach froths into an

unexpected sleep. I fade to ghost.

Every speculation of what happened on that particular evening in Paris
between the hours of 8:30 PM and dusk passes like exhaust over

my face.

Maybe he boarded the metro with me at Châtelet, followed me home to
Pantin, tapping his feet lightly on the snow behind me, but was too slow to

squeeze

into the complex. I must have locked the apartment gate so quickly
that the door's slam sounded more final than my clumsy fingers could

actually muster.

Or did he get off the train before me—my metro ride too long for his
liking: twenty-five minutes, when he only had fifteen to

get the job done.

Or maybe he never left the bar, never moved from behind the counter and got hard

just seeing me begin to crumple

on my stool only a quarter into my first and only Maredsous ale.

He might have handed me the drink while smiling at me, tickled by the quiet power of his finger, a dirty wand plunging into the hollow

of my thistle glass.

I'll never know exactly where the story starts. In which sip the sedative activated, when its hushed shrapnel exploded against

every soft pink wall of me.

That night, I went home and made an omelet. Burnt it till the apartment smoked up like the gates of hell.

Stumbled

to bed with my party clothes on and at 10:30, I was still confusing the collapse of my limbs for a weakness that was entirely my fault.

With every two hours that passed, I kept snapping the branches of sleep. Heard the winter wind hiss through the shutters.

Felt a fire around my pillow.

That night, I learned that danger had a heat. Passed closely to the face, buzzed and
snarled and took a couple of steps back, just to look at me in the eyes before

it did what it wanted.

But couldn't.

I must have locked the apartment gate so quickly that the door's
slam sounded more final than my clumsy fingers could

actually muster.

The next morning, I found my apartment key still in the door stuck stiff and deep

like a dagger in flesh.

What hand guided me through an evening of one thousand
almost deaths?

What bell clanged in my sternum like a call to the town square of my spirit?

From the indigo of that evening until the seagull grey of the
sky the morning after,

I sat up and lied down.

And sat up and lied down.
Like a drill. Like a torture.
Like a ritual. Like I knew how to break a spell.

Like something was being kneaded out of me.
Like I needed something to be out of me.

Like I already hated what would await me in the
back of my head and behind my eyes

if I let myself go.

Like even five years later and in America,
I'm still not snapping in and out of sleep,
searching for a word in any language to

define this stubborn pulse—

What do we call the woman that survives poison?

When she is returned to her memory,
and she is given back to her breath,
and she emerges from the silence of her vanishing—

Call me a woman who is just now learning how to accept how close
I was to falling into darkness.

Call me someone's failed project: a sharp light on evil.

Call me the flicker of sun between heavy eyelids.

Call me daybreak.

THREE DAYS BEFORE MY BAPTISM

For the past week, the knot housed in my womb
has thrashed against the inner wall of my stomach.

It is an always feeling. An anger spasms in my uterus
while I lie in bed. With every step that I take on my way

to wherever it is that I am walking, it juts out below my
belly button. I rub my middle in circles as if to find the

back of an intruder who wants to hurt me, but thinks I may
first owe it love. But hadn't this been my whole life?

I'd spent so much time caring for the things that burned
me in the places I didn't know how to soothe.

Or how to reach. Three days before my baptism, I find the
words to whisper a sacred goodbye. I shower, sloughing

off dead skin mixed with lavender soap from my tired body.

It leaves me, a spongy burgundy corpse that looks like velvet
cloth passing between my legs. It looks back at me, blinded

by thc shower's steam. I push it down with my toes through
the drain. I step on the face of a nightmare that is smaller

than my body, but bigger than time. Passed down from
shadowed hand to shadowed hand, imperceptible in the

charcoal bowels of my dreams, this is an ancient pain.

So old it has no name, so stubborn it traveled a century
to take hostage of my becoming. But my prayer is a furnace.

A flame runs down the back of a generational horror.
It loosens itself from my womb.

As I stomp, it scatters and runs toward the water.

ACKNOWLEDGMENTS

Poems included in *A Brief Biography of My Name* have appeared
in the following publications:
Vinyl Poetry & Prose and *Ledge Mule Press:* "Mother's Rules."
Entropy Mag and *Ledge Mule Press:* "Rekia and Oscar and All of
Their Sky Cousins."
Amazon: Day One and *Ledge Mule Press*: "I Ask My Brother
Jonathan to Write About Oakland, and He Describes His
Room."
Pop-Up Magazine: "Soumission Chimique."
Monster House Press Quarterly and *Ledge Mule Press:* "New
America."
Ledge Mule Press: "Space."